CLEVELAND RADIO PLAYERS

Published by Cleveland Radio Players

Copyright © 2015 by Jack Matuszewski

All rights, including the right of reproduction in whole or in part, in any form, including digital reproduction, are reserved. Published in the United States by Cleveland Radio Players.

CAUTION: Professionals and amateurs are hereby warned that *The Big Bad Wilf*, being fully protected under the Copyright Laws of the United States is subject to royalty. All rights, including professional, amateur, motion picture, recitation, lecturing, public reading, radio and television broadcasting, and the rights of translation into foreign languages, are strictly reserved. Particular emphasis is laid on the question of readings, permission for which must be secured in writing from the author's representative at Cleveland Radio Players, 2218 Superior Ave, Suite 203, Cleveland, OH 44114. The amateur acting rights of *The Big Bad Wilf* are controlled exclusively for the author by the author's representative.

Original adaption and Performances

Originally adapted for the radio and performed by The Cleveland Radio Players. Directed by Milton Matthew Horowitz. Recorded at Bad Racket Studios.

Starring:

| | |
|---|---|
| Denny Castiglione | The Voice of The Cleveland Radio Players |
| Logan Smith | Narrator |
| Charles Hargrave | Wilf the Wolf |
| Eric Sever | Little Red Riding Hood |
| Deanna Dionne | Grandma |
| Stefan Johnson | Woodsman |
| Andrew Jurcak | Copper #1 |
| David Flynt | Copper #2 |
| Denny Castiglione | The Real Narrator |

Screenplay

THE BIG BAD WILF
A COMEDY IN TWO ACTS
BY JACK MATUSZEWSKI

                NARRATOR
a whitty snarky lad with some tales
to tell

               WILF THE WOLF
a wolf if ever there was one only
Wilf is not ferocious at all

           LITTLE RED RIDING HOOD
A very tough little girl on her way
to grandmothers house

                GRANDMA
[PLEASEINSERT\PRERENDERUNICODE{ÂĂIJ}INTOPREAMBLE]GRANNY[PLEASEINSERT\P]
Red's febeal old grandmother

                WOODSMAN
the axe weilding woodsman who saves
the day and teaches lesons

               COPPER # 1
a police officer

               COPPER # 2
a second police officer

            THE REAL NARRATOR
the real narrator of the story

OPENING CREDITS

        THE VOICE OF THE CLEVELAND RADIO PLAYERS
Hello... This is the voice of The
Cleveland Radio Players... My name
is Denny Castiglione, ladies and
gentlemen,

                     OPENING FANFARE
and you're listening to The
Cleveland Radio Players performance
of The Big Bad Wilf... Written BY
Jack Matuszewski, Directed by
Milton Matthew Horowitz. Narrated
by Logan Smith

ACT I SCENE I THE NARRATOR'S PROLOGUE

CRACKELING FIRE
PAGES TURNING
SLOW MELLOW "OLD TIMEY" MUSIC?

NARRATOR
Ah Greetings friends! it's a true pleasure to have you here. Come, relax a bit by my fire side. make yourself comfortable... for I'd like to tell you a story... have you ever heard a REALLY good story? Can you think of those times when you were little and you sat by the fireside or in your grandfather or grandmother's lap and listened to a tale, so intently, that you could have been convinced of virtually ANYTHING? Are there some stories that you know that you can tell over and over again and people will continue to ask you to tell them? All of this blooms out of the very heart, meaning, and magic of stories. And what effect they have on all of us... our children included. So what is a story? Is it a simply a plucky collection of funny characters made to make children smile and laugh? Or is it a tale of woe and dread sent to rip bone-chilling fear into the minds of listeners so as to caution them against wrongdoing? Perhaps it is a comment on the philosophical goings on of the art, literature, culture, and politics of the day. Or perhaps still... it is all... and none of these. It is what our hearts and minds make of it. It is wherever our imaginations choose to take us on the wings of lions and talons of crows. So sit back. Enjoy yourself... as I regale you with a story

FADE OUT ALL

ACT I SCENE II WOLF AND RED

                     NATURE SOUNDS

      NARRATOR
so shall i begin begin our first story in the Deep Dark Forest. It is summer time here; a time for growing and maturing; Change and development. It is near the end of summer. A time when nature is no longer new and fresh yet is not ready to bear fruit. The plants and trees are yet under ripe and the farmers are still unsure if it will be a good harvest or not. So do we now meet our first player. He too is entering into a summer, rapidly growing, willing to bear fruit, but still uncertain of the vitality of his stocks. Let us hope for all our sakes that his, is a good harvest.

      WOLF
Hi everybody. Welcome to the Deep Dark Forest. I'm the wolf, The Big Bad wolf to be exact. Yes I know that contrary to my name I'm not very big. But just you wait and see. I can most definitely be bad!

                 WOLFS FEEBLE GROWLING

      WOLF
Oh who am I kidding!? I'm not big or bad! so here I sit in the Deep Dark Forest waiting for something to come by so that I could tear it into shreds and gobble it all up. That's right. That's why I'm here! A few days ago my dad took me aside and said to me he said (said with a deeper and more masculine voice) "Son, you've reached that very special age and... well I think it's time for you to maul your first little girl." But of course I was just all like, "Dad I don't want to maul anyone." And of course he just started going on and on about how it's a "wolf's duty" and the "glory of the hunt." But I just

                    WOLF
don't get it. I know that wolves
are carnivores. I mean, we have to
hunt in the forest and eat meat to
survive right?... but ya know?... I
hear that there are some places
where wolves live WITH the humans
instead of mauling them all the
time. Yeah! My cousin told me that
he heard about this one wolf who
gets to sleep all cozy and warm
next to a human's fireside and he
doesn't have to hunt for his food
and the humans give him a whole
bunch of different kinds of meat
and and he wears a shiny collar
with his name on it and everything.
But my dad would never let me do
that. I have to wait here so that I
can maul a little girl and carry on
the big bad legacy.

                    NARRATOR
while contemplating mauling little
girls ironically none other then
Little red riding hood would come
skipping into the woods, She sings
"la la las" stupidly as The wolf
gasps and hides behind a tree

                                    RED TRA-LALAS

                    RED
tra-la la la la la... Oh hello. My
name is Little Red Riding Hood

                                    RED GIGGLES INSANELY
I am taking some delicious goodies
to my grandmother who is horribly
insane and senile. She lives here
in the Deep Dark Forest. Although
why a physically feeble and frail
Woman would want to live here by
herself in the midst of bone
chilling and foreboding Woodland...
sure beats the heck out of me....
Oh well! My lot in life is not to
question but rather to follow
blindly and to smile in the face of
almost certain and horrifying
danger

                    SHE GIGGLES INSANELY
                                    RESUMING HER "LA LA LA'S"

WOLF
Ok here we go... remember what dad told me: Smooth but fierce, forceful but not rabid.

RED'S LA'S HAVE BECOME INCREASINGLY LOUD AND OFF KEY

WOLF
Grrr! Growl! snarl-

RED
La la la lalala

WOLF
umm...

RED
La La La!

WOLF
Excuse me!

RED
Lala lala LA!

WOLF
Excuse me!

RED
Lala lala la LLLAAAA!!

WOLF
HEEEYYY!!

WOLF
Ok, little girl, now see here! I'm a big bad wolf and-

RED
Oh look, how cute a PUPPY!....Daaaww! wook at da snuggy wuggy PUPPY! aw wook at his widdel face!

WOLF
Stop that! stop stroking my furr... your making my leg twitch stoppit...

RED
Aw, what's the matter puppy? Are you lost?

                    WOLF
What?... no I'm not lost I just
need-

                    RED
some food! I'm sure you're a very
hungry little puppy.

                    WOLF
Well actually... yeah. That's
exactly why I'm here.

                    RED
Of course it is! That's why your
dear sweet Red has a nice big thing
of corn for you

                    NARRATOR
She produces from her basket an ear
of corn, which she then proceeds to
shove into the wolf's mouth

                    RED
There you go, puppy! Eat the corn!
It's good for you!

                    NARRATOR
The wolf takes the abuse until he
finally smacks the corn away from
her

                    WOLF
Now look here you... you... Human
Female! I am not a puppy and I do
not eat corn!

                    RED
Now, puppy don't be silly and eat
your corn

                    NARRATOR
produceing yet another ear of corn
and forcibly places it in his mouth

                    WOLF
Hey! I said stop that! Listen. I'm
a big bad wolf see? And you're an
innocent little girl see? And I've
got to maul you to shreds, ya got
me? So don't make this any harder
than it has to be!

                    RED
That is so cute the puppy's trying
to be aggressive! Awwww!

                    NARRATOR
red begins violently petting him,
which makes his leg twitch

                    WOLF
NO!! Now listen you can either
submit and make this horribly gory
scene a little less gory or you can
be eaten while kicking and
screaming. It's your choice but I
should warn you that I feel no need
to be gentile just because you're a
sweet little girl. We big bad
wolves are-

                    RED
Oh, look at the time! I have to be
getting to my horribly withered and
decrepitly feeble Grandmother!
Tah-tah puppy!

                                        RED TRA-LALAS

                    WOLF
(really annoyed) Well isn't that
just perfect! Think of it. I
couldn't even scratch a helpless
little girl. Me! A big bad wolf!
What'm I supposed to do now?! Dad's
gonna kill me!... But ya know...
She wasn't all that bad. I don't
really want to hurt her. Yeah
right, as if I could! Now she's
just going to skip off to her
grandmother's house where.... ...
Wait a minute... What was that she
said about her grandmother being
feeble and decrepit? Hey! Why
couldn't I maul HER?! Yeah just
stop in, do a little mauling, and
then pop right out without even
touching any hooded little girls.
Then I can tell dad that the pride
of the big bad line is perfectly in
tact. Uh oh, I'd better hurry! I've
got to get to that grandmother
before some OTHER harmless woodland
creature eats her!

                                        FADE OUT ALL

ACT I SCENE III GRANNY'S HOUSE

FADE IN GRANDMAS HOUSE THEME MUSIC

NARRATOR
Ah yes! We come to a place that everyone knows. It is everything a child could want warm, nice and cozy, with the hearty scent of a freshly slaughtered woodland creature roasting on the fire. (he sniffs the air) mmm Is there any place more welcoming? "What is this place?," you might ask. Where else but Granny's House! And who should live in Granny's House but... Granny herself. You might not be able to pick up on it at first but... well let's just say that she is something a bit less... or should I say more?... than your average grandmother
Granny although she looks like your typical granny fitted in a cap and gown

GRANNY
Hello my dears!

GRANNY GIGGLES INSANLEY
welcome to... to... wait. Where am I? Oh yes, that's right, my house! I live here all alone, in the Deep Dark Forest, every day hope' in that I don't come across any... woodland creatures. Oh but I manage. I pass allot of the time by cooking. Of course I don't always have the exact ingredients that I need, but I do just fine by improvising. Ya see all ya gotta do to be a good cook is to know how to improvise! Why just the other day I ran out of bacon so's all I did was substitute it with skunk meat. And then, the cow wouldn't give me any milk so I just drank a bucket of pig's milk!

KNOCK ON THE DOOR

                    GRANNY
I wonder who that could be.

                                        KNOCKS AGAIN

                    GRANNY
Im comin Im comin...

                                        DOOR CREAKS OPEN

                    GRANNY
now I could have sworn I heard some
body a knock' in on my door!

                    WOLF
     (indignantly) Ahem!

                    GRANNY
Oh I'm sorry. I didn't see ya
there. (to the side and very
depressing) Of course I don't
really see much of anything any
more any way (she does yet another
insane laugh and is instantly back
to light hearted again) come on in
then sweetie. (she forcibly pulls
him into her house) And what might
your name be?

                    WOLF
Well... uh... wolf?

                    GRANNY
Huh? What was that? These great big
ears I have don't really hear very
well.

                    WOLF
I said wolf!

                    GRANNY
Huh? wolf?... hmm... is that short
for Wilber or wolfred?

                    WOLF
no, no, not wolf. wolf!

                    GRANNY
Oh well that's very nice young
wolf! How very kind of you to come
visit me like this. Here have a
seat.
wolf

No I really-

                                                        THUD

             GRANNY
Now I know how hungry you grow' in
boys can get-

             WOLF
(ominously) You got that right-

             GRANNY
So I'll just fix ya up something
nice.

                                                   DISH SHUFFLE

             GRANNY
That there soup is good eat'n!

             WOLF
look... uh... Granny, you've been
really nice and all but to tell you
the truth I didn't really stop in
for a friendly visit. I'm actually
here to... um... well... gobble you
all up.

             GRANNY
Huh? What was that?

             WOLF
I said I'm here to gobble you all
up!

             GRANNY
Huh...gobbeldy soup? Oh! You want
some Gobbeldy soup aye? I'm afraid
I don't have any Gobbeldy soup
right now. But I yeh know I could
make some for ya if ya wanted. As a
matter of fact I just got some
chicken feathers and pig hooves the
other day so I could whip some up
in a jiffy!

             GRANNY
I haven't made gobbeldy soup since
Edmund caught that wild chicken
with his pet gopher... it's so good
when ye cook it right... I haven't
had the chicken feathers for
gobbeldy soup yeh see?...

                    WOLF
Granny just listen... ok I don't
want any more soup... no be
careful... watch out... not
there...

                    WOLF
Granny!

                    GRANNY
the trick to a good soup is
stirring it just right with a
wooden spoon

                    WOLF
Granny!!

                    GRANNY
and just when you think you stirred
it enough you gotta stir it a
little more

                    WOLF
GRANNY!!

                    NARRATOR
and for a moment Granny stopped as
if she could hear the Wolf

                    WOLF
Look Granny. I know you can't hear
very well but I'm going to speak up
and I want you to listen very, VERY
carefully I know you just wanted to
be nice but I did NOT just drop by
for a friendly visit. I do NOT want
any gobbeldy soup. And I am NOT
wilf. I'm a wolf!

                    GRANNY
WHAT?!

                    WOLF
I said I'm a wolf!-

                    GRANNY
A Wolf?..... AHH!

                                                FIGHTING

                    NARRATOR
all of a sudden out of nowhere
granny produced a broom and began

NARRATOR
to beat The wolf helplessly. he ran about the house recklessly trying to cover himself from Granny's broom. when suddenly-

CUT FIGHTING

KNOCK AT THE DOOR

NARRATOR
another knock at the door interrupted the beating

GRANNY
(calling) Come in!

RED
Granny!

NARRATOR
Granny then ran to Red and they held each other in a tight embrace as granny said-

GRANNY
Oh, my dear... who are you?

RED
Granny it's me. It's Red

GRANNY
Oh yes of course RED... Come in come in... there's someone i want you to meet... Now, Red dear... I would like you to meet my friend... umm... I'm sorry what's your name again honey?

WOLF
umm... wolf?

GRANNY
ohh thats right... wolf!?

RED
wolf?

GRANNY AND RED
WOLF!!!

FIGHTING

                    NARRATOR
Granny and Red then magically drew
brooms from no where and
simultaneously chase and beat the
wolf while he frantically tried to
flee

                    WOLF
Wait! Stop! Please!

                                        CUT FIGHTING

                    WOLF
Look, look I don't really want to
hurt anyone!

                    RED
you're lying!

                                        FIGHTING

                    WOLF
no! wait! Please!

                                        CUT FIGHTING

                    WOLF
I really don't want to hurt anyone!

                    RED
then why did you come to granny's
house hmm?

                    WOLF
ok I'll admit it. I did want to eat
your grandmother-

                    GRANNY
I knew it!

                                        FIGHTING

                    WOLF
But! BUT!

                                        CUT FIGHTING

                    WOLF
I don't anymore! I just came cuse I
was told I had to.

GRANNY
What?

WOLF
Well ya see, my dad thinks that all wolves have to be mean and constantly maul people all the time. But I don't believe that. All I've ever wanted was to just live with people and NOT hurt them.

RED
(skeptically) Really?

WOLF
Yeah! Honestly! Don't get me wrong I love living in the woods and all, but sometimes I just think of what I wouldn't give to curl up next to someone's nice warm fire.

GRANNY
You know, I do get rather lonely in this deep dark forest with nothing to protect me from those... evil squirrels. Would you like to stay here?

WOLF
Could I?

RED
well that depends... I can't have just any crazy old hound looking after my granny!

WOLF
Oh I could make it worth her while!

RED
Really? Will you help me to go hunting for dinner?

WOLF
Sure! Will you scratch behind my ears?

GRANNY
Oh most definitely! But will you keep my feet warm on cold nights?

               WOLF
Can do! But will I get to eat
something other than skunk meat?

               RED
*sigh* alright... I GUESS!

               GRANNY
Well then it's settled. I let wilf
stay here with me and he no longer
has to maul innocent people.

               RED AND WILF
yay!

               NARRATOR
just then a Woodsman  burst in.

                                    DOOR KICK IN

               NARRATOR
He held an axe over his shoulder
and was panting.

               WOODSMAN
 Granny, Red. Sorry I'm late but I
guess better late than never right?
Well... let's get this over with

               NARRATOR
the woodsman then raised his axe
over his head aiming it at wolf.

                                    GRANNY SCREAMS

poor wilf doves behind her skirts
as Red threws herself between them

               RED
Hey!.. who are you!?

               WOODSMAN
Who am I? I'm the Woodsman, girly,
Q.E.D.

               RED
Woodsman? we don't need any
Woodsman! and don't call me GIRLY!

               WOODSMAN
Listen, GIRLY, the story NEEDS a
Woodsman at the end. So here I am!

GRANNY
What're you doing here?

WOODSMAN
Oh for the lova- don't tell me you don't know the story. Alright everybody listen up! This is how the story goes, and it can't be changed so don't even try!: the wolf talks to Red, then he goes and eats grandma, then he's about to eat Red when I come in and save the day.

RED
Save the day huh?

WOODSMAN
Yeah!

GRANNY
So... how does one... "save the day" exactly?

WOODSMAN
Well that's simple. All one need do to save the day... is just... uh... kill the wolf of course

RED, GRANNY, AND WILF
KILL THE wolf?!

NARRATOR
just then as if by magic wolf produces a third broom and he, Granny, and Red beat and chase the Woodsman screaming

NARRATOR

Things aren't always as they appear are they? All dogs were once wolves. That's right even your sweet little schnookums who would never hurt anybody. wolf may not have been the best wolf but he was one of the best friends an old lady like Granny ever had. He never did get a chance to maul anyone yet his failure as a beast was the beginning of a triumph for all dogs. He set a new standard for man and beast to be able to coexist. Oh

                    NARRATOR
          I'm sorry  act one is over. It's
          intermission now. We have to set up
          for the next act. So go on! Get up!
          Stretch your legs... get something
          to eat, maybe talk about how you
          liked if if you want. Oh but don't
          pick it apart too much... cus after
          all... it's only a story.

                                          FADE OUT ALL

ACT II SCENE I THE BOY WHO CRIED WOLF

                                FADE IN EARLY MORNING MUSIC

                    NARRATOR
          Welcome back everyone. Did you
          enjoy your stretch? Good. Back to
          the story then. now this story is a
          little different from the first one
          ya see... but we might see some of
          the same characters show up so
          don't worry about having to learn
          anything new... ya see that makes
          things easy on you which makes
          things easy on me... its not easy
          tellin these storys ya know... they
          don't just let anyone tell these
          stories... you know what I had to
          do to get this job... now where was
          I oh yeah act two... its about a
          shepards boy who's only job was to
          watch over a flock of sheep...
          sounds like a simple task sure
          enought but watching sheep graze
          can get boaring... so well ya get
          what we have here...

                                           FLOCK OF SHEEP

                    THE SHEPHERD BOY
          gahhhh.... I hate watching this
          stupid flock of sheep... there's no
          wolfs around here... I'm 12 years
          old and I've never once seen a wolf
          in my life...

                    NARRATOR
          With eyes slowly glazing over, he
          sat back, reclining himself against
          a tree... and heaved a great sigh

                    THE SHEPHERD BOY
Hhhuuuuhhhh....

                    NARRATOR
Lazily, he began to bemoan his
predicament

                    THE SHEPHERD BOY
MAN, i'm Bored! why do I have to
watch the stupid sheep? just caus
i'm 12 now everybody says i have to
"accept stupid responcability."

                              SHEPHERD BOY YAWNS
aaahhh... but that's dumb... this
is ALL dumb. and i'm TIRED let's
face it i've never seen a wolf and
i'm never GONNA see a wolf...
hmmm... where could i take a nap
out of sight?!... oh, Duh! the
haystacks!

                    NARRATOR
And what do you think the young man
with new and important
responcability did?.. why he went
directly over to the haystacks,
flopped directly into the middle of
the softest one, and fell fast
asleep.

                              SHEPHERD BOY SNORING
Fast asleep but not long asleep.
for just as he had made himself
comfortable...

                    WOODSMAN
well what have we here?

                    NARRATOR
the woodsman came strutting along
by

                    WOODSMAN
what's this? the shepherds post
stands vacant? where is the
sheapherd's boy?

                    NARRATOR
soon the boy's snoring would lead
the woodsman to the very haystack
he was sleeping under

WOODSMAN
Now see here BOY! ... wake up!

SHEAPHEARD BOY STOP SNORING

THE SHEPHERD BOY
what... huh?....

WOODSMAN
Rise and shine Sheapheard Boy... what do you doing sleeping on the job?

THE SHEPHERD BOY
aww what does it matter?...

WOODSMAN
what does it matter?... why you wouldn't say that is a wolf ran off with your sheep now would you boy?

THE SHEPHERD BOY
Well thankfully there's no wolfs within 1000 miles of this place...

WOODSMAN
ok maybe your right... but what if your wrong... what if there is one... just lerking out of sight... waiting for the lazy Sheapherd boy to fall asleep so he cn sneak off with you sheap one by one... and before you realize what happened all your sheep have been picked off.... and you and your family and villiage have no meat or sweaters to survive the cold weather...

THE SHEPHERD BOY
awe that's never gonna happen

WOODSMAN
it's never going to happen because you going to stand watch like your told and take your job seriously or well find a new sheapard boy and send you off with the lumberjacks to heft axes into trees all day... now stand you POST!

NARRATOR
and off he struted after standing the shepard boy up and scolding

                    NARRATOR
him, the woodsman returned to uh
well doing woodsman stuff while the
boy was left to wallow in his own
anger...

                    THE SHEPHERD BOY
how embarrasing... who does that
woodsman think he is... he's not my
dad... he can't tell me what to
do... I'll show him... we'll see
who's afraid of the big bad wolf...
tomorrow morning you in for a treat
woodmans

                    NARRATOR
you can't see it the shepherd boy
is making scheeming face right
about now... a childish and
obnoxious plot was brewing in his
bratty little head and well like he
said the next morning as soon as
the rooster crowed

                                        COCK A DOODLE DOO

                    THE SHEPHEARD BOY
wolf... wolf wolf.... I see a wolf

                    NARRATOR
that's right you see where this
story is going... the boy cried
wolf for petes sake!

                    THE SHEPHERD BOY
It's a wolf ... It's a wolf I tell
ya I see a wolf

                    NARRATOR
The woodsman heard the boys cries
and grabed for his Axe

                                             AXE SOUND

                    NARRATOR
the town crier began to ring the
church bell

                        BELL TOWER RING
                                        FADE IN ANGRY MOB

NARRATOR
people from all over the small
village began to flock to fields
the shepherd boy tended but when
they arrived

WOODSMAN
where... where is the wolf boy

THE SHEAPHERDS BOY
oh I uh I guess he uh must have
been scared off?

WOODSMAN
well you did see a wolf then didn't
you? did he take off with any of
the sheap?

THE SHEPHERD BOY
um no he didn't but he was big and
scary just like you said he would
be...

WOODSMAN
uh huh... well good work boy...
keep tending to post then as you
were...

NARRATOR
now the woodsmand wasn't sure if
the boy was telling the truth or
not but a few hours later when her
heard

THE SHEPHERD BOY
wolf... wolf... I see a wolf!

NARRATOR
and again the woodsman grabed for
his Axe

AXE SOUND

NARRATOR
and the crier rang the bell

BELL TOWER RING

FADE IN ANGRY MOB

NARRATOR
and the villagers flocked to the
fields, only to be met with

THE SHEPHERD BOY
hahahaha... sorry he must have gotten away again...

WOODSMAN
now look here Sheapheard boy... I would hate to think that you were having a laugh at the villages expense by yelling wolf when there clearly is NO wolf...

THE SHEPHERD BOY
what?... who me?... why would I do something like that... hay how do you know I didnt see a wolf lurking in the shadows just like you said...

WOODSMANS
I warn you boy if you cry wolf again there better well be a wolf on the prowl for if there isn't I assure you that you will be punished

THE SHEPHERD BOY
okay but I think we scared him off for good this time so we probably won't be seeing him again...

NARRATOR
but wouldn't you know it, dear friends, JUST before sundown, as thw woodsman was just about to call it a night. he opened his window and heard-

THE SHEPHERD BOY
Wolf!... wolf... oh, WOLF! i really DO see a wolf!... i deffinately DO this time!

NARRATOR
and for the third and most exausting time in one day the woodsman picked up his axe

AXE SOUND

the crier rang the church bell

BELL TOLLING

and all the villagers came running, at once to help the poor Shepherd

NARRATOR
boy, who they feared was being
attacked!

WOODSMAN
Now that just does it, boy! for the
THIRS and FINAL time i have come up
here and for the third and final
time i see NO WOLF!

THE SHEPHERD BOY
WAHAHA! oh REALLY?! no wolf, eh?...
hehehe... and i wonder why THAT
could be?

WOODSMAN
what the Devil are you talking
about, boy?!

THE SHEPHERD BOY
oh, just how silly you all look...
hahaha... scrambeling across the
hill... hehehe... trying to "save
me" from something that isn't
there!

WOODSMAN
Well now that just tears it! there
is no wolf here and all these times
you've been shouting, to wake the
dead, and there's never been a wolf
has there?!

THE SHEPHERD BOY
HA! now, at last, you're getting
it... NO! that's right. there IS no
wolf, there's never been a wolf,
and there will NEVER be a wolf

WOODSMAN
now, look here-

THE SHEPHERD BOY
no YOU look! i've been sitting here
ALL DAY... and fer what? fer
NOTHIN! there ARE NO WOLVES. i got
here at sun up, did nothin, sat
around, did EVEN MORE nothin, and
now that it's sun down, i'm just
like, thinkin, like... what have i
even been DOING here?!... NOTHIN!

24.

> WOODSMAN
> Boy! i have told you before-

> THE SHEPHERD BOY
> No, woodsman! i wasted a whole day! and do YOU see any wolvese here?.. huh? so, ya know what? it's gettin dark. i should be gettin' to bed...

> NARRATOR
> and with theat the Shepherd Boy arrogantly strolls off... and the woodsman well the woodsman was quite steemd about the whole thing so he thought to himself for a moment and came up with the bright idea to scare him straight he thought

> WOODSMAN
> Hay... I know how to teach that kid a lesson... didn't Granny just get a new live in wolf... yeah... last time I seen that old ding bat she was chasin me out of her house with a wolf and a little girl brandishing brooms... I wonder... I wonder if they might help me...

> NARRATOR
> and of course Granny and Wilf... uh I mean wolf would agree to help the woodsman... I mean what else do they have goin' on? its an old lady and a wolf all alone deep in the woods... so any way back at Granny's house

ACT II SCENE II BACK AT GRANNYS HOUSE

> KNOCK ON DOOR
> GRANNYS HOUSE THEME MUSIC

> GRANNY
> I tell ya Wilf sometimes these old houses are drafty

> KNOCK ON THE DOOR

> WOLF
> Granny I think someones at the door

GRANNY
whats that wilf?... it's even windier then before?

KNOCK ON THE DOOR

WOLF
No granny someones nocking on the door

GRANNY
your right is even windier then before... mabye have a look and see out the door here

CREAKING DOOR OPEN

oh why hello Woodsman... didn't know you were here... Why didn't cha knock?

WOODSMAN
Granny... I came here to ask you and your pet Wilf for help

WOLF
Wolf!... and w-w-why would a wooodsman need the help of a wolf?

GRANNY
he's right why would a tool man want to play golf?

WOODSMAN
we've had a problem with the Shepherd Boy in the village... He keeps crying wolf when there is no wolf, and well I would like to put an end to that and I need your help...

WOLF
w-w-what would I do?

WOODSMAN
Well you are a wolf arnt you?

GRANNY
of course his names Wilf why do you think we call him that?

WOLF
My name is WOLF and yes I am but maybe you haven't noticed but Im not very big or bad at all...

WOODSMAN
and thats why I need your help... I dont really want to put the Shepherd boy in any danger and most of his stuborness is due to the fact that he has never seen a real wolf...

WOLF
You mean... I would be the first Wolf he ever saw

WOODSMAN
Thats right

WOLF
and he would actually be scared of me?...

WOODSMAN
well from a distance I dont see why not... ya see what I want you to do is lurk in the shadows and peek out at him every once in a while... let his mind play tricks on him... then dart out and grab one of the sheep and run back to the edge of the forrest... place the sheep in pen I will build out of sight... and one by one I want you to pluck off all his sheep

WOLF
b-b-but wont the the young shepard boy scream for help

WOODSMAN
I'll take care of that too... I will wake up extra early and make the rounds in the village to make sure nobody comes to help the shepherd boy when he cries wolf... he needs to learn that nobody believes a lier even when their telling the truth.

WOLF
Ok I'll do it but you gotta promiss you wont reach for your axe

WOODSMAN
I give you my word...

                    WOLF
and the crier wont ring the bell?

                    WOODSMAN
I'll see to it that not a single
toll will ring all day

                    WOLF
and the villigers wont assemble
leagly and dmonstrate thier legal
right to assembly?

                    WOODSMAN
no mob shall rise ill see to it
myself... trust me... the villagers
are as crossed as I am with the
Shepherd Boy...

                    WOLF
Ok mr woodsman you have yourself a
deal...

                    GRANNY
you want me to cook another
meal?... well ok I guess I have
some more soup I could stir up....

                    NARRATOR
and stir up some soup Granny would
indeed... and the woodsman, Garanny
and wolf would have some soup and
iron out their plans for the next
day...

                                             FADE OUT ALL

ACT II SCENE III THE SHEEP FIELDS

                    NARRATOR
now the next morning in the fields
the Shepherd Boy showed up his
usuall lazy self and was
considering napping in the hastacks
again when he thought to himself

                    THE SHEPHERD BOY
hmmm... I wonder if the woodsmans
had enough... if I take a nap in
this hay is he gonna come scold me
about responsibilty or will he just
leave me alone

NARRATOR
just as the shepherd boy began fluff the hay out of the corner of his eye is spoted somehting darting from tree to tree in the shadows

THE SHEPHERD BOY
wait a minute... is that... no way... it couldn't be...

NARRATOR
just then wilf peekd his snout out from the shadows showing nothing but his teeth

THE SHEPHERD BOY
oh my gosh... it's ... it's a real w-w-w-wolf...

NARRATOR
and before he could scream it Wilf dashed out into the field and grabbed on the the sheep at the far end of the field...

SHEEP SOUNDS

THE SHEPHERD BOY
WOLF!!!....

NARRATOR
only this time the woodsman wouldnt reach for his axe...

THE SHEPHERD BOY
WOLF!.....

NARRATOR
and the crier didn't ring the bell...

THE SHEPHERD BOY
WOLF!... does any one hear me?! there really is a wolf

NARRATOR
no villagers would come to the shepherd boys cries... and the wolf would grab all the sheep and place them safely in the pen the woodsman build out of sight... and when the last sheep was finally gone

                    THE SHEPHERD BOY
why... why didn't the woodman come
with his axe... and why didn't the
church bells toll when I called for
help... surely some of the villages
had of herd me... oh man... my
dad... is gonna be so mad... and we
dont have any meat for the winter
or wool to make sweaters...
w-w-what am I gonna do oo ho ho
hoooo

                                SHEPHERD BOY CRYING

                    NARRATOR
and just as the shepherd boy began
to weep who would come runnin up
witha broom but Granny

                    GRANNY
Oh Hello Shepherd boy I heard ya
screamin wolf from deep in the
woods and I grabbed my broom and
came a runnin... wheres that big
bad wolf Ill show him a thing or
three about snatchin our sheep...

                    THE SHEPHERD BOY
it's too late granny... he already
made off with all the sheep...

                    GRANNY
whats that boy?... ya got cold
feet? well put some socks on why
dont cha... here I might have and
extra pair here...

                    THE SHEPHERD BOY
no Granny I dont need Socks ...
wait how did you hear me screamin
wolf from across the village and
you cant hear me from two feet
away?

                    GRANNY
yes I know you have two feet just
hold on a minute... now where did I
put those extra wool socks

                                      DISTANT LAUGHTER

NARRATOR
just then the woodsman and the rest of the villages would appear from behind a hill laughing and leading the sheap back to the field safely

THE SHEPHERD BOY
wait...w-w-whats going on here....

WOODSMAN
hahahah well we had enough of you cryin wolf so we decided to play a little joke at your expense...

THE SHEPHERD BOY
but the wolf he was real... I saw him...

WOLF
oh ya mean me?

THE SHEPHERD BOY
you're the wolf? but you look more like... a dog... I was so scared I lost the whole villages sheep... I'm sorry I didn't take my job more seriously...

WOODSMAN
hahaha well sometimes it takes a whole village to raise a boy right...ya see Wilf and the crier and the villagers and the sheep were in on it the whole time...

THE SHEPHERD BOY
and Granny too

WOODSMAN
no actually I have no idea how she got here Granny... how were you able to have a hand in this

GRANNY
whats that? you want me to fix you some sandwiches? well allright but I dono if i have enough ingredients for a whole village but Im' sure I cn whip somethin' up...

NARRATOR
and granny would whip something up for the whole village... I don't

                    NARRATOR
          know if that last part is true but
          lets just pretend it is...

                                             FADE OUT ALL

FINAL SCENE

                         CRACKLING FIRE
                           PAGES TURNING
                                  SLOW MELLOW "OLD TIMEY" MUSIC?

                    NARRATOR
          and well there ya have it...
          another story told and another
          notch to add to my belt... well...
          it's gettin' late here in story
          land and it's about time for me to
          punch out, so I'll just uh mosey on
          out of here and leave you to
          remince with your feelins...

                         FOOT STEPS
                                             DOOR BURSTS OPEN

                    REAL NARRATOR
          HEY! there's the guy officers...
          that's the guy who knocked me out
          and stole my suite and
          microphone... somebody stop him

                    NARRATOR
          oh crap you brought the law? time
          to scram...

                                             FOOT CHASE

                    REAL NARRATOR
          Grab him don't let him get away!

                                             TACKLE/BODY THUMP

                    COPPER # 1
          Oh he's not go'in no where

                    COPPER # 2
          yeah where do you think you're
          goin'... no where thats where...

                    WOODSMAN
          Alright, alright. What's all this
          noise about... who's this man in
          his underwear here?

> REAL NARRATOR
> That man! He beat me up and took my cloths and microphone... and he stole my oldish looking Narrator book... give that back!

> WOLF
> woodsman?... are you Ok in there whos that man talking about oldish looking narrator books?

> REAL NARRATOR
> It's the book that contains all the stories in Storyville and it belongs to me... I was suppose to be the narrator of this show... THAT!... is an impostor!

> FULL CAST GASP

> NARRATOR
> Well of course that's preposterous! I'm no impostor... the word impostor implies I'm a phoney and why just look at how well I told this story.

> REAL NARRATOR
> Well?! HA! This has to have one of the most bazaar fairy tales anyone here as ever heard! Big bad wolves living with old ladies, sheep plotting with wolves... It's lunacy I tell you lunacy!

> RED
> Can you believe this?

> GRANNY
> Did he say some thing about a fake Narrator?

> THE SHEPHERD BOY
> how Bizarre...

> NARRATOR
> You don't understand! You needed me! Do you know what this story could have been? Huh? Do yah? Pixy dust and dew drops that's what! Rosy cheeked children giggling and waving. Can you even imagine?-

REAL NARRATOR
Well not any more we can't you impost-a-narrator !

NARRATOR
ok, ok fine! It was bizarre! but not as bizarre as that pun you just made... So maybe I'm not legaly a narrator in storyville but Im not the worst

COPPER # 1
look we dont take kindly to any rogue narrrators illeagly narrating withing storyville limits without a licens

COPPER # 2
yea the sherrif of storyville has us cracking down all over the place...

NARRATOR
But have I not accomplished something great here tonight? These people... have they not laughed? Have they not questioned themselves just a bit? All I wanted to do was to just try and change the world... even if just in the slightest way-

REAL NARRATOR
News flash buddy! You don't do that by kicking the crap out of a guy and then tying him to a 300 lbs light board backstage.

RED
Oh dear!

GRANNY
How incredibly barbaric

NARRATOR
If you take me out now you'll regret it for the rest of the story!

WOODSMAN
I think we've heard just about enough out of you Mr. fake narrator... wouldn't you agree half dressed guy?

                    THE REAL NARRATOR
Absolutely...but not before he
gives me back my suit and
microphone ok get him outta here
boys.

                    COPPER # 1
sir if you would come quitley with
us your under arrest for
impersonating a narrator

                    COPPER # 2
thats right storyville has strict
rules about story time shenanigans
involving false representaions of
would be storyville characters

                    NARRATOR
No! you can't! I'll resist you!
You'll never stop the story... it
plays on and on and on until we
wake up!

                    GRANNY
(softly crying a bit) look away
wilf, look away...

                    THE REAL NARRATOR
He's gone off the deep end boys...
have him fitted for a straigh
jacket

                    NARRATOR
no! NO! never! Not me! Not the
story! You can't end the story like
this! I will not be finished in
such a way! I am all! I am the
story! Aaaahhhhhh!

                              NARRATOR KICKING AND SCREAMING

          RED
So if that was the wrong
narrator... did we just listen to
the wong endings to our stories?

              THE SHEPHERD BOY
what do you mean "wrong ending" now
we have the right narrator here! So
how do the stories end Mr.
NARRATOR!

REAL NARRATOR
well... it doesnt work like that...
I dont know!

WOODSMAN
you don't know?! You're the
Narrator! Of course you know! Now
come on! Tell me!

WOLF
Is wolf ever forced to maul anyone?

WOODSMAN
What do the Woodsman 's future job
prospects look like?

THE SHEAPHEARD BOY
do I ever meet a Shepherd girl?

RED
Oh yea do I ever run into a handsom
prince in the forrest?

REAL NARRATOR
Listen!... That's not how stories
work... He already told the end
it's too late I cant change it

RED
how can the Narrator not change end
of his own story?

REAL NARRATOR
Cus it's not my story anymore... if
he told it

GRANNY
What?

REAL NARRATOR
wilf could have just as easily
eaten Red. and if the shepherd boy
had just been honest Wilf never
would have come at all. There are a
million different ways the story
could have ended but it ended the
way it did because that's the way
he told it... or wrote it

GRANNY
Great! Now we'll never have endings
to all our stories!

REAL NARRATOR
I'm sorry everybody... but it just isn't my job to finish other peopls stories... I just tell them...

WOLF
Well then... if you dont write them... who does?

REAL NARRATOR
hmm... Maybe you?...

WOLF
Me?!

REAL NARRATOR
Yes you... And maybe also them.

WOODSMAN
who?

REAL NARRATOR
those who may have heard this strange story here tonight, and wants to hear more... Anyone can tell a story, but it takes a creative mind to write a story not everyone can do it but maybe you could... or one of them out there...

RED
what do you mean?

THE SHEPHERD BOY
Yeah! so is writing these stories?!

THE REAL NARRATOR
I'm trying to tell you YOU can add you OWN page to the Book of Storyville.

THE SHEPHERD BOY
the Book of Storyville? what in the Wilf, is the Book of Storyville?

WILF
Hey-

REAL NARRATOR
Why it's the very tome I hold here in my hand, my young fellow.

WOODSMAN
oh, yeah? so what's so special about it?

REAL NARRATOR
ya see this book is comprised of stories sent into us here at Storyville. all the greatest tales go into the book to become stories that are told... forever

GRANNY
what do we have to do to make sure people remember us

WOLF
or remember our stories?

REAL NARRATOR
All one needs to do to keep the stories alive is share them.

WOLF
and sharing that story might inspireothers to share their own

GRANNY
Old Glory? I remember old Glory it was a great story

RED
A great story still needs an audience Granny...

REAL NARRATOR
that's where I come in... if anyone, even those, listening now, believes they have a truley amazing tale to tell... they can write it down, send it in to me, and If... it is indeed worth the telling... you may one day hear me telling your story! and if it's told once... maybe it will be told again. and if it does... well, who knows? it may verywell be told again and again forever.

END CREDITS

>                    THE VOICE OF THE CLEVELAND RADIO PLAYERS
>           you have been listening to The
>           Cleveland Radio Players Performance
>           of The Big Bad Wilf... Written by
>           Jack Matuszewski... Directed by
>           Milton Matthew Horowitz...
>           STAEEING...

                    CUTLER SMITH
CHARLES HARGRAVE

                    ERIC SEVER
DEANNA DIONNE
BEAU REINKER
GIOVANNI CASTIGLIONE
ANDREW JURCAK
DAVE FLYNT

>           And my name is Denny Castiglione
>           Ladies and Gentlemen... The Big Bad
>           Wilf was recorded Live at Bad
>           Racket Studios... copywright 2015

Rights and Royalties

Originally adapted for the radio and performed by The Cleveland Radio Players

Directed by Milton Matthew Horowitz

Recorded at Bad Racket Studios

For more information on performance rights and royalties, or to listen to The Big Bad Wilf as a radio play, please visit
www.ClevelandRadioPlayers.com